Echoes of My Space

My Space: A Journey Towards Self-Discovery

25 Poems And Their Quotes

&

Reflections

By Divya Shiji

Title of Your Book: **Echoes of My Space**

Copyright © 2024 by Divya Shiji

Disclaimer: This book is a work of fiction. Names, characters, places, and incidents are products of the author's imagination or are used fictitiously. Any resemblance to actual events, locales, or persons, living or dead, is entirely coincidental.

Author's Website: **https://myspace20.in/**

For more information, contact:
divyashale@gmail.com

Acknowledgment

I would like to extend my heartfelt gratitude to all those who have supported me throughout the creation of this book, "Echoes of My Space."

First and foremost, I want to express my deepest appreciation to my Lord Almighty for guiding me every step of the way. I am immensely grateful to my parents, my Papa and Mumma, for their unwavering love, encouragement, and understanding. Their support has been my rock throughout this journey.

To my beloved family, my Achachan, and my kids, Ashale and Oshana, thank you for being my constant source of inspiration and strength. Your presence in my life fills each day with joy and purpose.

To all the readers who embark on this poetic voyage with me, thank you for your time and for allowing my words to touch your hearts. Your support means everything to me.

Lastly, I want to express my gratitude to everyone who, knowingly and unknowingly, has helped bring my vision to life and given me the courage and strength to pursue my passion despite the challenges.

This book is a testament to the power of community, love, and the written word. Thank you, from the bottom of my heart, for being a part of this incredible journey.

Heartfelt Regards,
Divya.

"Poetry is the echo of the voice of the soul."

Sarah Josepha Hale

"In the quiet moments of everyday life, I find the truest expressions of my soul, where words become the echoes of my thoughts."

Divya Shiji

Welcome to "Echoes of My Space."

Within the pages of this book, you will embark on a journey through the corridors of my mind, where every verse is a whisper of my soul and every line a reflection of my heart's cadence. These poems are the echoes of my deepest thoughts, crafted with ink dipped in the inkwell of introspection.

I am not a professional writer, but within these words lies the essence of my being. They are born from the raw emotions and unfiltered truths that pulse through me. As I navigate the labyrinth of life, I am continually reminded that my thoughts are not just fleeting whispers—they are profound teachers, imparting invaluable lessons with each passing moment.

Many of these poems originated from my website; My Space: A Journey Towards Self-Discovery https://myspace20.in/, where I first began to explore and express my innermost thoughts. Now, I gather the strength to compile them into this book, "Echoes of My Space," to share with you.

Each poem is a mirror, offering glimpses into the labyrinth of self-discovery and the gentle embrace of self-love. From the quiet moments of solitude to the crescendo of resilience, this collection is a testament to the human spirit's capacity for growth, healing, and transformation.

Accompanying these verses are carefully curated quotes, like guiding stars in the night sky, illuminating the path to understanding and enlightenment. They serve as companions on this poetic voyage, echoing the sentiments and wisdom found within these pages.

May these words resonate with you, stirring the echoes of your thoughts and emotions. May they inspire you to embrace your journey of self-discovery, finding solace and strength in the beauty of introspection.

Welcome to "Echoes of My Space," where every word is a melody and every page a sanctuary for the soul.

Let our journey begin...

Table Of Content

Vanish To Observe

In shadows deep, I yearn to hide,
A day of disappearing, unseen beside.
No eyes shall glimpse my presence near,
But mine shall witness, crystal-clear.

A silent specter, a ghostly guise,
I'll wander through the world's unseen skies.
Eavesdropping whispers, secrets untold,
Unveiling truths that were once withheld.

I'll hear their words, the tales they weave,
What do they say when they think I've left?
A mirror reflecting their thoughts, uncovered,
A lesson awaits, to be unchained.

A space where once I played,
No laughter was shared, and no memories were made.
Yet the pang of sadness may never fade,
Deep within, a longing stirs.

To be missed, to matter, as it were,
Today is a canvas, a chance to explore.
I'll dance with the wind, sing with the streams,
Unburdened by judgment, I fulfilled my dreams.

Life will carry on; no one will notice,
But in my heart, a transformation is born.
To change or be, the choice is always mine,
On this day of vanishing, there is a chance to shine.

So, as I fade from their view, unseen,
I'll relish the joy, pure and serene.
In my absence, I'll truly be
A moment of respite, just for me.

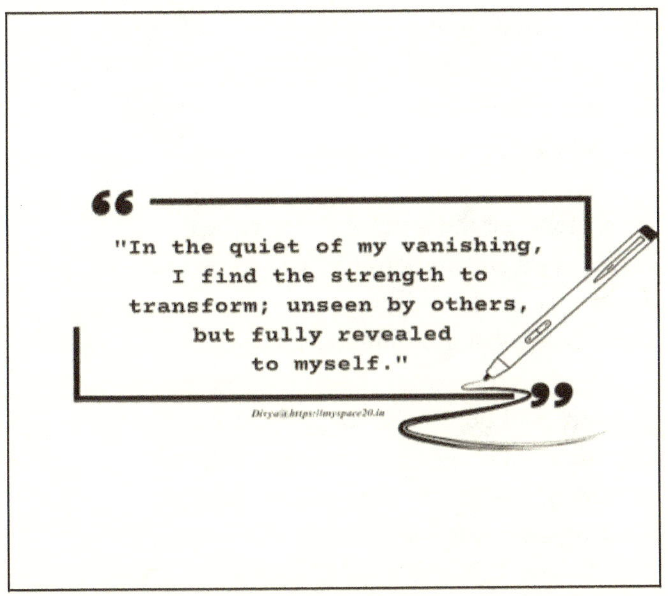

P.S. *This poem is a reflection of my imagination, a journey into the realm of vanishing and observing my absence. Through these words, I planned to convey the essence of disappearing into the shadows, seeking solace in the unseen, and discovering the profound truths that emerge in moments of quiet observation.*

A Beautiful Lie

In the kingdom of words, I shall now weave,
A poem for you, to ponder and perceive.
About the question that we all hear,
"How are you?" whispered in our ear.

Often, we reply with a simple claim,
"I'm good," we say, making the frame.
But deep within, a battle may reside,
The truth we hide, with a smile behind.

For sometimes, the weight of life we bear,
Leaves scars and burdens too hard to share.
Yet, in this lie, there lies a spark,
A tiny flame that glows in the dark.

This beautiful lie, a balm for the soul,
A gentle push to help us reach our goal.
It murmurs, "You can step up and can try,
Though you're not fine, spread your wings and fly."

The question itself, a catalyst to motivate,
Igniting embers of hope, despite our state.
But the answer we give, a secret pact we make,
To find strength within, for our own sake.

So let the question inspire, and the lie propel,
As we navigate this journey, all is well.
For in this dance of truth and pretense,
We find the courage to face life's immense.

So when asked, "How are you?" every day,
Remember the choice to choose your own way.
To utter the words that push you to strive,
And keep the flame of hope alive.

P.S. *I wrote "A Beautiful Lie" to express how I feel when someone asks me, "How are you?" Even when I'm going through tough times, I often say, "I am fine." This poem reflects the mixed emotions I have in those moments, where I hide my true feelings behind a polite answer.*

Teach The Heart To Smile

Within my smile, a day so bright,
But tears can turn it into night.
The choice is mine, to laugh or weep,
My day's reflection, mine to keep.

I choose to smile, to find delight,
Though deep within, my heart takes flight.
It laments throughout the day,
Haunted by pains that won't decay.

To teach my heart, a daunting quest,
To guide it toward eternal zest.
Like a carefree child, pure and free,
To dwell in joy, perpetually.

It took time for my heart to see,
The path to childlike jubilee.
But as it learned, a wondrous thing,
Great days ahead, joy's song would sing.

Each day I cherish, come what may,
By embracing joy, all fears allay.
For in my heart, a smile's embrace,
Transforms each moment with sweet grace.

So let me revel, day by day,
In laughter's light, worries allay.

A childlike heart, now full of glee,
Living in joy, eternally.

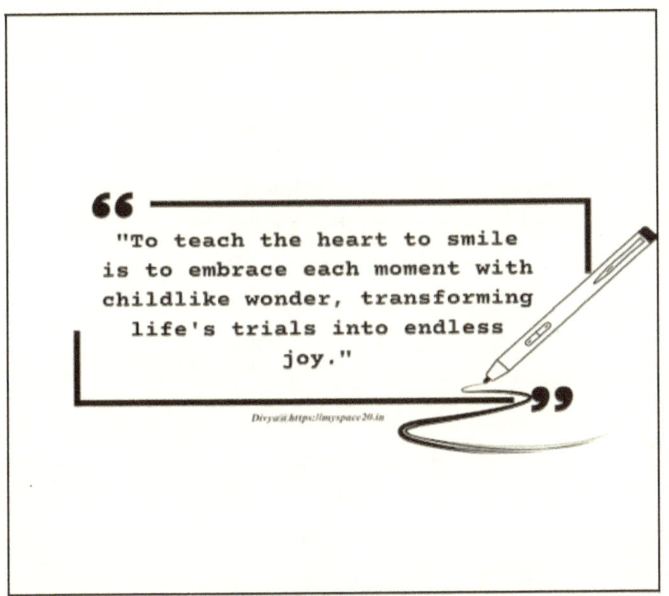

P.S. *I wrote "Teach The Heart To Smile" as a reminder to myself and others that joy is a choice we make each day. Amidst life's inevitable challenges and sorrows, I believe we have the power to shape our experiences by choosing to find delight in the small moments. This poem is my commitment to nurturing a heart that embraces happiness, no matter the circumstances, and to inspire others to do the same.*

Count the Sorries

In words so simple, let me convey,
A tale of sorry, day by day,
A word that holds immense power,
To mend hearts, in every hour.

When deeds go wrong, and faults arise,
Sorry emerges under a humble guise,
A bridge we build, to heal the strife,
A chance to change and transform life.

Through humble lips, it finds its way,
An admission of mistakes, we say,
A promise made, to make amends,
Walk anew, where darkness ends.

It cools the anger, like gentle rain,
Easing tension, soothing the pain,
A balm for souls, in conflict's wake,
A chance for harmony to partake.

In every word we speak, we find,
The need to say, "I was unkind,"
For Sorry teaches us to see,
The value of empathy is set free.

From the first words to our final breath,
Sorry, companion till death.
Yet we speak without thought,
Unaware of lessons left untaught.

So count the sorries, one by one,
Reflect on the days when they were done,
A mirror to our hearts, it shows,
The growth path, where kindness grows.

In gratitude, we find our grace,
Sorry too, deserves a place,
For in its essence, we can find,
The seeds of change are within our minds.

Let sorries guide us, hand in hand,
To better lives, where we will stand,
And may we learn, from each regret,
To be the best that we can get.

So cherish your sorry, and use it wisely,
To mend the wounds, that pain belies,
For in its simple, humble words,
Lies the power to be seen and heard.

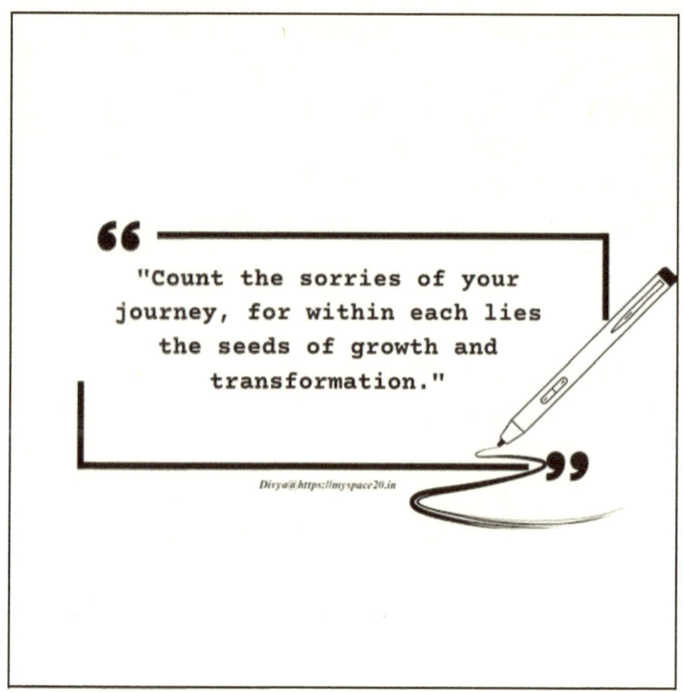

P.S. *I wrote "Count Your Sorries" to highlight the importance of acknowledging our regrets and mistakes as essential parts of our personal growth and transformation. Each "sorry" we experience is a lesson, a step towards becoming a better version of ourselves. This poem serves as a reminder that our journeys, with all their imperfections, are valuable and that embracing our sorries can lead to profound self-discovery and change.*

Why to Compare?

In a world so vast, where uniqueness thrives,
Why compare ourselves, lead burdened lives?
For what I possess, they may never find,
And what they hold, I may not desire in kind.

In smiles that bloom, each a personal tale,
There is no need to tether or scale.
For joy knows no bounds, no limit to share,
So why compare, and seek a burden to bear?

The melody of life, a symphony unique,
Each note is a reflection of the soul we speak.
In dreams, we chase, aspirations untamed,
No need to compare, no need to be tamed.

Our paths diverge in myriad ways,
Different passions fuel our numbered days.
What brings me to tears, may not touch their hearts.
Our journeys, dear friend, are worlds apart.

Embrace diversity, let comparisons cease,
Celebrate beauty and find inner peace.
For in our differences, lies strength untold,
United we stand, our spirits bold.

So let us break free from the chains that bind,
Embrace the essence of our own design.
Why to compare and why to compete,
In this vast tapestry, find solace, find a treat.
We are unique, like stars in the sky,

Let your light shine, soar, and fly.
Embrace your journey, let comparisons fade,
In this vast mosaic, let your true colors cascade.

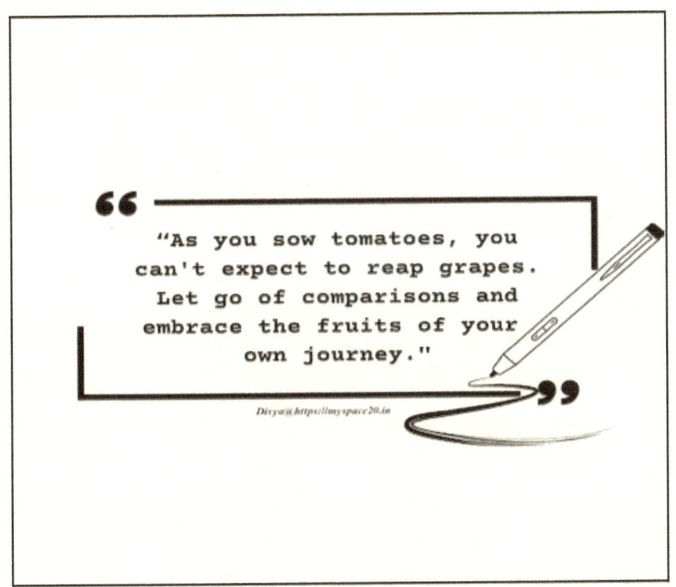

Note: *Dedicated to all caring parents, who sometimes find themselves caught in the cycle of comparison. As parents, it's natural to want the best for our children. However, comparing them to others can diminish their self-worth and hinder their personal growth. Let go of the burden of comparison and instead provide a nurturing and supportive environment where your child can thrive.*

Whispered Words

In the morning's golden light so bright,
A mother's voice called with all her might,
"Baby, it's time to rise and shine,
The day awaits, it's a gift divine."

But the little one lay in slumber deep,
Unaware of the tasks she had to keep.
Once more, the mother gently implored,
"Get up, my baby, let your dreams be stored."

Then, something wondrous filled the air,
A soft whisper came from a heart so fair.
With determination in her little voice,
The daughter spoke, making a choice.

"Come on dear, it's time to wake,
Many things today I need to undertake.
I'll rise with a smile, like a shining sun,
Embracing the day, getting tasks done."

The mother, amazed, asked her daughter why,
She spoke to herself with that heartfelt cry.
The daughter smiled and began to explain,
Her words held wisdom, free from any strain.

"Amma, your words gave me strength, it's true,
But my affirmations made my spirit anew.
They filled me with power, bright and strong,
Believing in myself all day long."

In that moment, a lesson was learned,
The power of simple words, how they yearned,
To ignite a flame within our souls,
To help us achieve our lofty goals.

So, let us remember, in every single day,
To speak words of love in our own unique way,
For simple words hold the power to inspire,
To uplift, encourage, and set our hearts on fire.

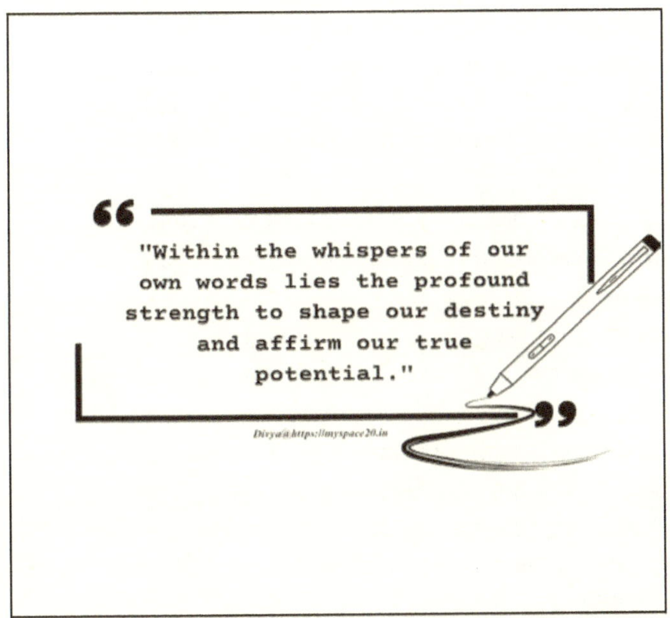

P.S. *I wrote "Whispered Words" to capture the profound impact that words of encouragement and self-affirmation can have on our lives. The poem reflects the dynamic between a mother's nurturing words and a child's realization of their own inner strength.*

The Beauty of the Word Beautiful

In a world of innocence, a little girl's mind,
She saw the word "beautiful" as one of a kind.
To her, it meant only looks, appearances, and charm,
A shallow view, causing hearts to harm.

With eyes wide open, she judged by the face,
Unaware of the depth, of each unique grace.
She yearned to be beautiful, like a flower in bloom,
Unaware of the beauty that dwelled in each room.

But as time passed by, her wisdom did grow,
She learned there was more to this word, she now knows.
Beautiful, a word with a soul so vast,
A treasure within, when the moments are cast.

Beauty in laughter, brightening up the room,
Beauty in kindness, sweeping away the gloom.
Beauty in strength, standing tall and proud,
Beauty in love, so profound and loud.

The word transformed, like a butterfly's flight,
From mere superficiality to a radiant light.
She realized that beauty lies deep within,
In hearts, in minds, where true treasures begin.

Now, she sees beauty in the twinkle of an eye.

In the warmth of a smile, reaching for the sky.
In the embrace of a friend, through thick and thin,
In the resilience of a spirit that won't give in.

Oh, the beauty of "beautiful," she sings,
In all its forms, it spreads its wings.
No longer confined by narrow beliefs,
She celebrates the beauty that brings relief.

So, let us remember, like the little girl's view,
That beauty is diverse, in every shade and hue.
For the word "beautiful" holds a power so grand,
Embrace its true essence, hand in hand.

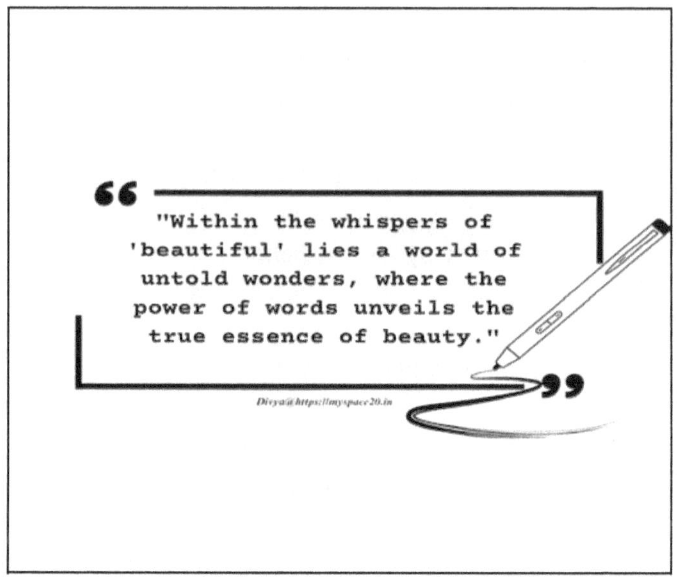

Note to Parents:

Discover the enchanting poem "The Beauty of the Word Beautiful" and embark on a journey of understanding with your children. This heartfelt piece encourages you to look beyond superficial appearances and embrace the true essence of beauty. Teach your children the importance of kindness, compassion, and empathy, as these qualities reflect the deepest beauty within. Let the power of this poem inspire meaningful conversations and foster a sense of wonder in your family. Explore diverse forms of beauty and celebrate the unique qualities that make each person shine. Nurture your children's self-esteem and help them appreciate the beauty that resides within themselves and others. With "The Beauty of the Word Beautiful," you have a precious opportunity to shape their perception of beauty and create a positive impact in their lives.

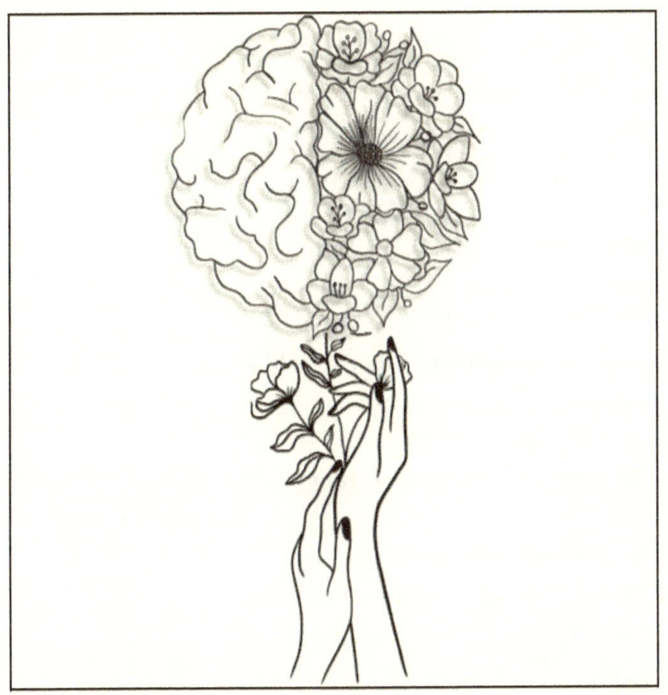

My Richness

"I Am Rich, And I Can Define My Richness."

In the world where wealth does dwell,
I find a story I must tell,
Of riches not in gold or land,
But in the heart, where joy expands.

I am rich, I proudly say,
Not for treasures that others display,
But for the blessings that surround,
Each day, in every sight and sound.

In the mornings kissed by the golden sun,
I find wealth in the dawn's first run,
A symphony of birdsong bright,
Filling my soul with pure delight.

I am rich when laughter resounds,
Echoing through life's merry rounds,
Shared with loved ones, side by side,
Their presence, a wealth I can't hide.

In moments of kindness, big or small,
I find riches that truly win all,
A helping hand, a heartfelt smile,
Enriching lives mile after mile.

I am rich when passions ignite,
Fueling dreams that take flight,
Creativity's fire burning bright,

Guiding me through the darkest night.

In nature's wonders, vast and grand,
I find wealth as they gently command,
Mountains high and oceans deep,
Awakening a love I'll forever keep.

I am rich, for within my soul,
I embrace gratitude as my goal,
Contentment weaves a tapestry,
Of richness that sets my spirit free.

So, let the world define its measure,
With treasures sought for endless pleasure,
For in my heart, I proudly declare,
I am rich, beyond compare.

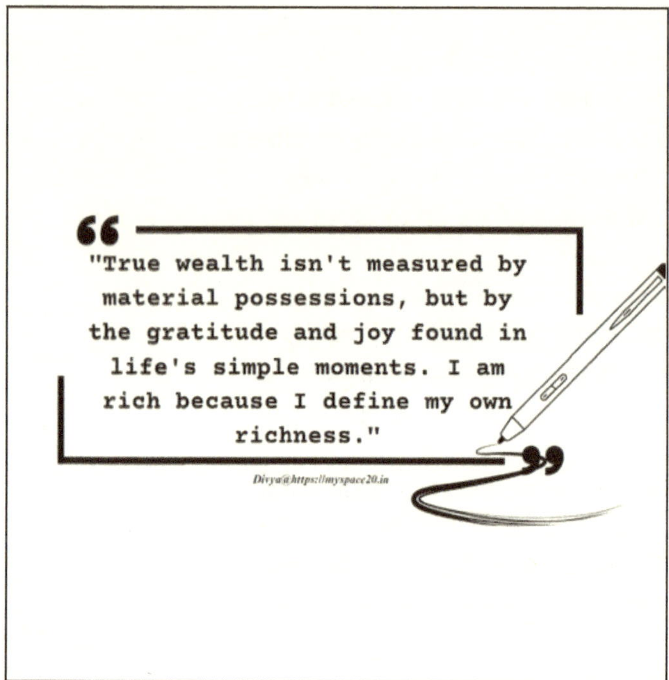

P.S. *I wrote "My Richness" to celebrate the intangible treasures that make life truly meaningful. In a world often focused on material wealth and external success, this poem serves as a reminder that real richness comes from the joy, love, and gratitude we experience every day. By recognizing and appreciating these blessings, we can find a deeper sense of fulfillment and contentment.*

Feel Your Feelings

In the depths of your heart, my friend so true,
Lies a precious gift, just for you.
Feel your feelings, listen to their call,
For they whisper secrets that will heal all.

When life grows heavy and burdens weigh,
Pause for a moment, let emotions have their say.
Acknowledge the sadness, embrace the joy,
Let your tears flow freely, let laughter employ.

Dear self, you're deserving of love and care,
Don't rush through life, but take time to repair.
Declutter your thoughts, let worries be released,
In the calm of your soul, find a moment of peace.

Empty yourself of stress, let it dissipate,
Replace it with hope, for it's never too late.
Recharge your spirit, let positivity ignite,
And in the darkness, let your inner light shine bright.

You are your own best friend, a confidant so dear,
Share your hopes and fears, with no hint of fear.
Feel your feelings, let them guide your way,
They'll lead you to a future filled with hope and sway.

So remember, my friend, in this journey you're on,
Feel your feelings, for they'll make you strong.
Understand your needs, and honor them with care,
For within your own heart, lies a world so rare.

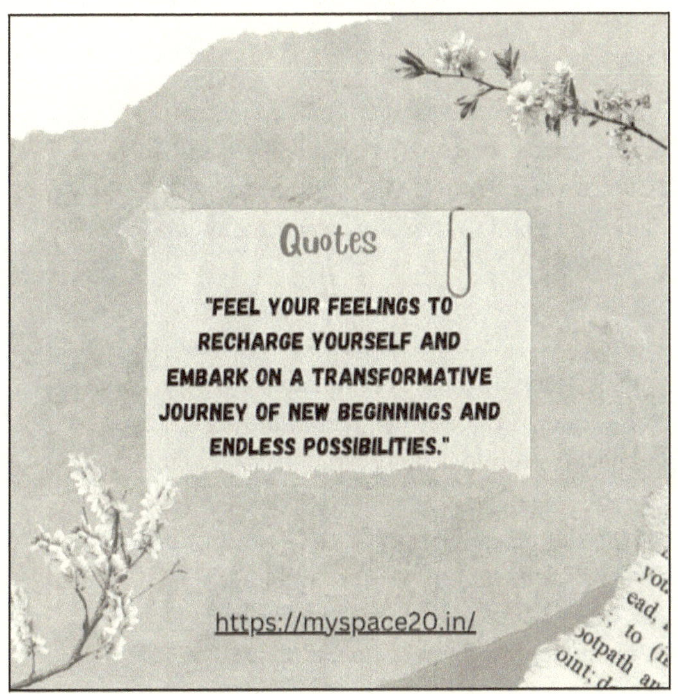

P.S. I wrote "Feel Your Feelings" as a gentle reminder to honor and embrace our emotions as integral parts of our human experience. In a world that often encourages us to suppress or ignore our feelings, this poem encourages self-awareness and self-compassion. By allowing ourselves to feel deeply, we open the door to healing, growth, and inner peace. May this poem serve as a guiding light for anyone navigating the depths of their emotions.

Goodness

"Don't Be Good To Showcase Your Goodness, But Be Good"

In a world that craves attention's sway,
Where deeds are done for accolades' display,
A voice whispers softly, so it's understood,
"Don't be good to showcase your goodness, but be good."

Let not your kindness be a mask you wear,
A superficial display, void of care,
For goodness true resides within the soul,
A beacon shining brightly, making you whole.

Be good, not seeking praises or acclaim,
But driven by a purpose beyond fame,
Let every act of love be pure and true,
With no agenda but to help and renew.

Let empathy guide you on this noble quest,
To see the world through eyes that truly rest,
On others' burdens, pains, and silent cries,
A genuine connection, no disguise.

For goodness springs from depths of selfless hearts,
From understanding every life it imparts,
And in its wake, it leaves a trail of light,
Illuminating paths, banishing the night.

Embrace the joy that selflessness can bring,

The boundless happiness that it can sing,
For in the act of giving, you shall find,
A beauty that transcends the passing time.

So let your actions be a testament true,
To goodness that resides and shines in you,
Don't seek approval or applause's nod,
But be good, my friend, simply to be good.

P.S. *"Goodness" was born from a reflection on the essence of true virtue in a world often dominated by superficiality and the pursuit of recognition.*

Ignore All Care And Complain; No One Cares

In this fast-paced world, moments go astray,
Unseen treasures slipping through the day.
The little things unnoticed, passing by,
They hold the unshed tears we let fly.

A stranger's smile, a wish so pure,
Lost in our rush, our sight unsure.
Let's pause and see the beauty that's there,
In each hello and every heartfelt care.

A mother's love, her cooking's embrace,
Nourishing our souls with every taste.
Yet we miss the flavors and the care she imparts,
Blinded by worries that cloud our hearts.

But let's not ignore the love that's there,
The sacrifices fathers silently bear.
Their fire burning strong, their love unseen,
Let's cherish the bond that lies within.

Grandparents wait, their patience so true,
Longing for connection, a love they pursue.
Their wisdom and stories, slipping away,
Lost in the chaos of our busy day.

Children's questions, innocence they bring,
Yearning for knowledge and understanding.
Let's not brush them off, but truly attend,
For these precious moments, let's comprehend.

Friends reaching out, seeking our embrace,
In this hectic world, they offer solace and grace.
Let's not ignore their calls, caught in our strife,
Connection is the elixir that brings life.

So let go of complaints, the "no one cares" plea,
The truth lies within, if only we'd see,
That in our negligence, we neglect,
The love and beauty around us, our souls' prospects.

Open our eyes, behold what's untold,
The small, unseen things that we've left cold.
In life's intricate details, love can be found,
If we pause, take a breath, and look around.

"We Ignored All Care And Constantly Complained that No One Cared, until we turned around and discovered that care was everywhere, filling the air with its silent grace."

My Need

In the depths of my soul, a Need resides,
Demanding and unyielding, it never subsides.
Since my birth, it has clung to me tight,
Always guided by others but now it's my own fight

As a child, my parents provided its care,
But now I'm grown, burdened by its snare.
It pressures me endlessly to achieve,
Yet its hunger is insatiable, I perceive.

Oh, Need, you're an enemy, relentless and strong,
Devouring my dreams consumes me wrong.
I yearn for freedom, to break your chains,
To find happiness where peace remains.

How can I control you, restrain your might,
And prevent you from engulfing my light?
I've lost so much in pursuit of your desire,
Leaving me empty, my soul worn and tired.

I beseech you, Need, let me be free,
Release your grip, please listen to me.
I long for a peaceful existence, serene and pure,
Where I determine my worth, my own allure.

But "Need" explains with its voice hauntingly clear,
"Just a moment, my friend, have no fear.
You cannot escape me, try as you might,
For without me, your world loses its light."

"I know I trouble you, cause you pain,
Yet you gave me the power to drive and step ahead.
You could have controlled me, tamed my fire,
But you let me consume you—your deepest desire."

Now you claim to abandon me, bid me adieu,
But deep down, you know it's not really true.
You're always with me, forever entwined,
In the journey of life, a bond is not defined.

Though I may trouble you and cause you strife,
Together, we navigate this journey called life.
Find balance, my friend, between need and desire,
And in harmony, forge a life you can admire.

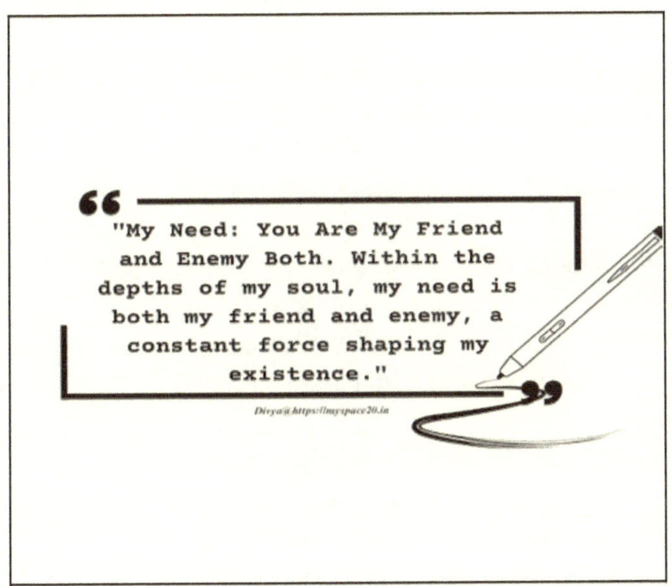

Choose Choices Wisely

In the orbit of choices, a power resides.
A tool that shapes paths where destiny hides.
In each moment, a decision is made.
A gateway to futures, both bright and gray.

Choice, oh choice, a double-edged blade,
Opening doors or sealing them with a fade.
A delicate dance, a precarious art,
To navigate life with a wise, mindful heart.

With every step forward, a choice to be made,
Forge a new path or follow the brigade.
Infinite possibilities, stretching wide and far,
Guided by the flicker of a distant star.

Yet in this dance, there's no foolproof guide,
No map or compass to sail the tides.
But don't fear dear soul, for within you lies,
The strength to discern truth from disguise.

When faced with a crossroad, a moment to pause,
Reflect on your values, embrace your flaws.
For the choices you make, they define your way,
Carving a story with each passing day.

And if ever you stumble, or take a wrong turn,
Know that resilience within you shall burn.
A chance to course-correct, to find a new light,
To rise from the shadows, reclaim what feels right.

So choose, dear friend, with a conscious mind,
Embrace the beauty of choices you find.
Even in darkness, a flicker of hope,
A chance to discover the strength to cope.

Choose wisely, with courage, let your heart lead,
Embrace the unknown, sow the seeds you'll need.
And as you journey through life's winding track,
May your choices bring joy, and never hold you back.

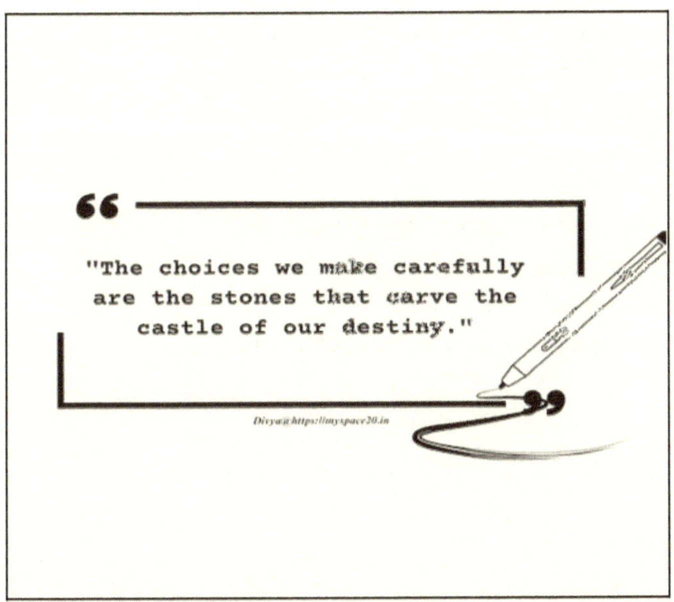

P.S. I crafted this poem to remind me of the ability to open infinite doors or close crucial pathways with my own choices.

Oh, My Baby Inner Me

Oh my baby inner me,
I hear your longing; I hear your plea.
Growing up can be a daunting ride,
But I'm here to be your guide.

Those moments we shared, so pure and true,
I wish I could bring them back to you.
Hold on tight, don't let go.
We'll find a way to let our spirits glow.

Amidst the chaos and demands of the day,
We'll carve out moments to laugh and play.
Together, we'll explore and rediscover,
The joys of life, like no other.

Embrace that childlike spirit within,
Let it bring you joy. Let it begin.
Oh my baby inner me,
You're always a part of me, eternally free.

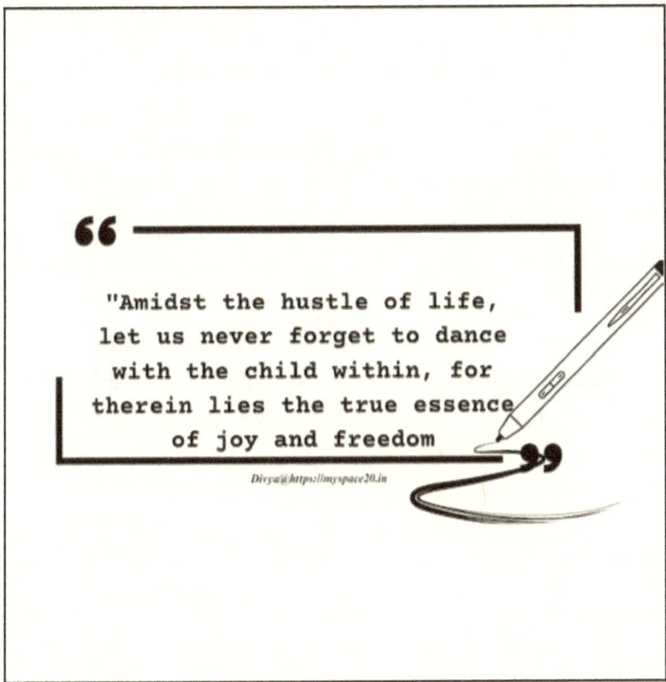

Divya@https://myspace20.in

PS: I wrote this poem as a reminder to myself, and to anyone who reads it, that no matter how busy or challenging life may become, it's essential to hold onto the innocence and wonder of our inner child. Amidst the responsibilities and pressures of adulthood, it's easy to lose sight of the simple joys and pure happiness that we experienced as children. This poem serves as a personal commitment to reconnect with that part of myself and to guide others to do the same, embracing the beauty of life with childlike wonder and enthusiasm.

I Am Enough As I Am

My Timeless Mantra

"I am enough as I am," my mantra, my creed,
No longer bound by others' expectations or need.
I refuse to alter, for their acceptance or acclaim,
With self-acceptance, my happiness will forever remain.

I'll rise above the doubts, no longer feeling small.
Embracing my worth and standing proud and tall
With self-love as my guide, I'll pave my own way.
"I am enough as I am" is the mantra I'll forever say.

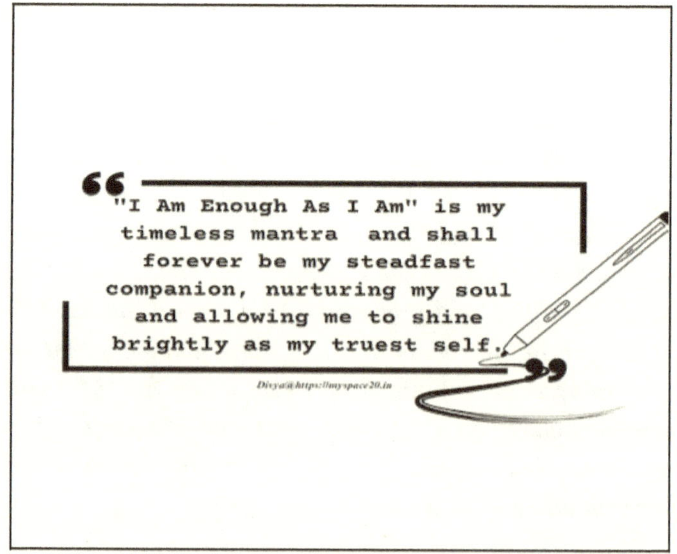

P.S. *"I Am Enough As I Am" encapsulates the empowering journey of self-acceptance and liberation from external validation. It speaks to the importance of embracing one's intrinsic worth and finding contentment within oneself. This poem serves as a declaration of personal empowerment and a reminder that true happiness stems from self-love and acceptance. May it inspire others to embrace their uniqueness and stand confidently in their own worth, knowing that they are truly enough just as they are.*

The Key To Control My Response

Today I feel the chaos in my soul,
As if everything's slipped out of control.
I cannot tame the swirling storm inside,
But in my darkness, a glimmering guide.

My mind consoles in gentle whispers,
"You're not a magician with answers,
To bend the world as per your desire;
But your response, dear, you can inspire.

Learn to control your actions and thoughts,
Train your mind to navigate the knots.
For in each challenge, there lies a chance,
To rise above and find a new stance.

Act with strength and purpose, don't tremble,
Let resilience help your spirit assemble.
Sometimes, through acting, we find our way,
Emerging stronger with each passing day.

Fear not the highs and lows that persist,
For within you, a key does exist.
Stay calm, dear one, and search deep within,
Unlock the solution, watch the problem thin.

PS: *I wrote this poem, "The Key To Control My Response," as a reminder to myself and others facing inner turmoil or external chaos. Sometimes, it's easy to feel overwhelmed by circumstances beyond our control. Yet, within that chaos lies an opportunity to harness our inner strength and shape our responses. By focusing on controlling our actions and thoughts, we can navigate through challenges with resilience and emerge stronger. This poem serves as a gentle nudge to trust in our ability to find solutions and persevere, even amid uncertainty.*

Whispers of Loss Overcome

In the depths of a sorrow's well, I once found myself
lost,
A battle within, a silent tempest, at great cost.
A loss that whispered, ever so softly, in my ear,
But I vowed to stay strong, show no signs of fear.

Yet clever was this loss, cunningly it conspired,
To slowly weaken my spirit, and make me tire.
Day by day, its whispers grew louder, it seemed,
But I refused to surrender; my hopes gleamed.

Then, like a divine blessing, love's echoes arrived,
Resounding with a fervor that kept me revived.
They drowned out the whispers, those echoes were so
clear.
I couldn't help but rejoice, banishing all my fear.

Oh, how wondrously God has woven this grand plan,
Guiding us through moments that we cannot withstand.
With the sword of love, we can conquer our despair,
Transforming whispers of loss into echoes rare.

This tale is not mine alone, it's a shared plight,
Every soul must navigate the shadows, seek light.
Don't let the whispers engulf and make you drown,
Find the echoes of love, and rise above with a crown.

PS: *"Whispers of Loss Overcome" was penned as a testament to the human spirit's resilience in the face of sorrow and despair. Inspired by personal experiences and observations, I crafted this poem to reflect on the journey from darkness to light, from whispers of loss to resounding echoes of love. It serves as a reminder that even in our darkest moments, there is hope and strength to be found in the embrace of love and the guidance of a higher power. This poem is a beacon of encouragement for anyone grappling with their own struggles, urging them to seek out the echoes of love that can uplift and empower them to rise above adversity.*

Eternal BFF's

Oh time, why don't you stay with me?
I long to be your dearest friend, you see
But you never consider me, it seems
I want to be with you in all your schemes

To comfort and reciprocate, my aim
But you always leave me; it's such a hurricane
In a hurry, you constantly reside
While I strive to be by your side,

You're punctual, never staying for a while
I need you, but you never seem to dial
So I'm making a new friend, you see
One who will keep you and me in harmony

Allow me to introduce Memory's name
She's my new dearest friend, and we're the same
You, Time, may be too busy and fleet
But Memory helps me recall when we meet

She brings back moments we shared as two
Moments of happiness, just me and you
So, Time, I'll continue to walk with you
Though I may falter, my efforts are true

And now, I am joyful beyond compare
We are friends forever, a perfect pair
Time, Memory, and I, united in glee
Forever enjoying life's journey, you see

P.S. As *I penned "Eternal BFFs," I reflected on the bittersweet joy of revisiting old memories through Google Photos every day. It's a poignant reminder of how swiftly time passes, slipping through our fingers like sand. Yet, amidst this transient journey, memories remain steadfast, ready to transport us back to cherished moments. Have you, too, experienced this nostalgic embrace of the past?*

A Yell for Freedom: To Be Me

I Yell for Freedom

I yell for freedom from everything
That holds me back from being me.
I want to explore myself,
To take time to know myself,
To care for myself,
To love myself.

I want to be free of expectations
Of the others,
From the labels they put on me,
From the roles they want me to play.
I want to be free to be myself,
Unique and individual,
Unafraid to be different.

I want the freedom to make my own choices,
To follow my own path,
To live my own life.
I want to be free and be happy,
To be content,
To be at peace with myself.

I yell for freedom,
For the freedom to be me.

I know that freedom is not easy,

That it takes courage and strength.
But I am ready to stand for it,
To be the one I was meant to be.

I am worthy of freedom,
Of being myself.
I will not give up,
I will not give in.

I will yell for freedom,
Until I am free.

P.S. *This poem was written as a declaration of self-liberation and empowerment. It was born out of a deep desire to break free from societal expectations, to embrace individuality, and to reclaim the right to live authentically. It serves as a reminder that freedom isn't just a concept but a journey—one that requires courage, perseverance, and unwavering self-belief. This poem was penned to inspire others to find their voice, to stand up for themselves, and to pursue the path of self-discovery with unwavering determination.*

In Search of a Friend

In this vast world where friendships bloom,
I search for a friend, but find only gloom.
Why is it so hard to connect and relate,
To find someone who mirrors my own state?

I've traveled far and met countless faces,
Yet none have reflected my inner spaces.
For friendship, they say, is a mirror fair,
Reflecting thoughts and feelings without a care.

But alas, this treasure eludes my grasp,
Each encounter is only a fleeting gasp.
I am a good speaker, a listener too,
A comedian, a teaser, all things I do.

But where is the one who truly understands,
Who sees me as I am, with open hands?
I've decided now, though the journey will be tough,
To be my own friend, that's more than enough.

I know myself well, every secret and fear,
No need to express in front of others so near.
So on this Friendship Day, I raise a cheer,
To my best friend, my true self, so dear.

Happy Friendship Day to me, I declare,
In my solitude, I'm not aware
Of the emptiness that once did sting,
For now, I embrace the joy it brings.

No need for another's reflection to see,
For I am my own friend, forever free.
In myself, I've found a loyal ally,
A companion true, till the end, I defy.

PS: *"In Search of A Friend" is a poignant reflection on the journey of seeking companionship and connection in a world where genuine friendships can sometimes feel elusive. Through this poem, I explore the complexities of human relationships and the longing to find someone who truly understands and accepts us for who we are. Ultimately, it's a celebration of self-discovery and self-acceptance, as the protagonist realizes the profound bond they share with their own self. This poem serves as a reminder that while friendships with others are valuable, the most important relationship we can nurture is the one we have with ourselves.*

Be Unique

Think out of the box, so trending these days,
Everyone strives to be unique in their own way.
But, my friend, before you step outside,
Know what's within you and the secrets you hide.

Explore the box, gather strengths and flaws,
Your weaknesses, your strengths—know them all.
When you think with confidence and grace,
You'll understand how the box contributes to chasing
your dream.

Be unique in your thoughts; think out of the box,
But first, be special; within its walls, unlock.
Plan accordingly, armed with knowledge inside,
Let your ideas fly with the box as your guide.

So remember, my friend, think both in and out.
Unleash your creativity beyond any doubt.
With the box as your ally, you'll surely succeed.
Then, think out of the box, and unique ideas will sprout.

P.S. *This poem was written to remind us that true uniqueness stems from understanding ourselves fully, both our strengths and weaknesses. It emphasizes the importance of introspection and self-awareness as the foundation for creative thinking. By embracing who we are within the confines of the box, we can then confidently explore new horizons and think innovatively outside of it.*

Soul's Odyssey

When I was a child, I was at peace,
Innocence and wonder never ceased.
Dreams unknowingly knocked on my door,
And stay with me forever more.

Peace was the essence of my being,
A calm state that kept me from running.
But as I grew, my fantasies evolved,
Complicated desires slowly resolved.

Dreams bought into my desire,
A ceaseless battle to ignite the fire,
Of becoming who I longed to be,
Expanding the territory of my destiny.

And so the day came when I finally arrived,
Who I wanted to be, my dreams contrived.
But these greedy desires were never satisfied,
Hungry for more, stress gradually amplified.

No further expansion; I cannot go,
Stress overtook me, inhibiting my glow.
Replacing dreams with who I wanted to be,
Lost in chaos, my spirit is not free.

Now that stress rules me, I struggle to find a way,
To reclaim the peace that once held sway.
After being with everyone, I learned a lesson:
Peace was the essence of my being.

So once again, I embark on a quest,
To nurture peace, find solace and rest.
Stress refuses to leave, a relentless foe,
But as I navigate this cycle, my heart does glow.

This eternal cycle completes every beat,
Between peace, dreams, and stress, I find my seat.
I strive to reclaim the peace of my youth,
Letting it guide me as my spirit seeks truth.

P.S. *I wrote this poem, "Soul's Odyssey," as a reflection on the journey of self-discovery and the cyclical nature of life's struggles and triumphs. It encapsulates the longing to return to a state of innocence and peace while acknowledging the inevitable influence of desire and stress as we navigate through life.*

Whispers of My Frozen Moment

In moments of serenity, oh! I wish time would freeze.
To relax in the joy that fills my heart with ease,
But alas! I know this can never be true.
In life's cycle, we must go on through

Yet still, a part of me yearns to hold tight.
To cherish that moment in its dazzling light,
Oh! I wish I could freeze just a bit more.
And taste the feelings that my soul adores.

In that precious hour when everything is clear,
Where happiness dances, banishing all fear,
I find meaning and purpose, a sense of delight,
Oh please! Won't you freeze this moment just for
tonight?

On a rollercoaster of emotions, I ride
Thoughts swirling within, like a turbulent tide,
And with this setback, I hesitate to go on.
Longing for a pause, a chance to prolong

Oh! Life, won't you grant me a freeze-frame embrace?
So I may live fully in this cherished space,
Within this moment, I find all I need,
A symphony of joy, a heartfelt creed

But as time marches forward, I must accept
The ups and downs of life intersect.
Though I crave that stillness, that pause in the flow,
I must journey ahead and let new chapters unfold.

So I'll treasure that moment like a precious gem.
In the depths of my heart, I'll hold onto them.
And with gratitude, I'll cherish each day.
Knowing that life moves on in its own special way.

P.S. *I wrote this poem, "Whispers of My Frozen Moment," as a reflection on the bittersweet nature of life's fleeting moments of joy and serenity. In moments of tranquility, there's often a yearning to freeze time, to hold onto the beauty and happiness that surrounds us.*

Oh, My Problem!

Oh my problem, you come each day,
I try my best to push you away,
But you always stand in my way,
Avoiding you is not an easy play.

I come up with tricks to greed you,
But then you trick me, like a mirage that's true,
We play hide and seek, me and you,
Always finding each other, it's nothing new.

Are we friends or enemies, I can't say,
For you're always there, come what may,
Could it be that we've found some kind of bond,
A peculiar connection that will forever respond?

Now I can call myself an artist, you see,
Facing you each time, it becomes a part of me,
From this constant battle, a lesson I gain,
oh problem, you're always here to remain.

So I embrace you, and I'll never depart,
For facing you is truly an art,
I've come to accept that you'll never leave,
But through facing you, I can achieve and achieve

P.S. *I wrote this poem as a reflection on the ubiquitous presence of challenges and obstacles in life. Through personifying the "problem" and exploring its dynamic with the narrator, I wanted to convey the universal experience of grappling with difficulties. The poem celebrates the resilience and growth that come from confronting problems head-on, transforming them from adversaries into opportunities for learning and self-discovery. It's a reminder that embracing challenges can lead to personal development and artistic expression.*

Give & Get Thanks

Give thanks and get thanks—a beautiful word,
In life's grand moments, let it be heard.
First, learn to give thanks for all that you owe,
Embrace every blessing, big or small, you owe.

Then learn to get thanks, as gratitude grows,
Find joy in the appreciation it shows.
Reflect on the moments when others may lack.
The treasures you possess, and give thanks back.

A cycle, revolving through each passing day,
In gratitude, find your own way.
For in the act of giving, you shall receive,
Abundance unbounded, beyond what you believe.

So, give and get thanks, with an open heart,
Let gratitude's magic ignite every part.
For in this dance of thanks, beauty is found,
A life full of blessings, forever profound.

P.S. This poem was written as a gentle reminder of the transformative power of gratitude. In a world often filled with distractions and challenges, it's easy to overlook the blessings we have and the opportunities to express appreciation. "Give & Get Thanks" aims to inspire a deeper awareness of the reciprocal nature of gratitude—that by giving thanks, we not only acknowledge our own blessings but also uplift others, fostering a cycle of positivity and abundance. So, amidst the hustle and bustle of life, may this poem serve as a beacon of mindfulness, guiding us to cultivate a spirit of gratitude and enriching our lives with its enduring beauty.

Dear Readers,

As you reach the end of "Echoes of My Space," I want to take a moment to express my deepest gratitude to each and every one of you.

Thank you for allowing my words to accompany you on your journey, for embracing the emotions and reflections woven into each poem. Your support and encouragement have been the driving force behind this collection, and I am truly honored to have shared a piece of my heart with you.

May these poems continue to resonate with you long after you close this book, offering solace, inspiration, and a reminder of the beauty found in the everyday moments of life.

With heartfelt thanks,

Divya Shiji